Celebrate
Buddhist Festivals

Series editor: Jan Thompson

Clive and Jane Erricker

Heinemann

First published in Great Britain by
Heinemann Publishers (Oxford) Ltd
Halley Court, Jordan Hill, Oxford OX2 8EJ

MADRID ATHENS PARIS FLORENCE PRAGUE
WARSAW PORTSMOUTH NH CHICAGO
SAO PAULO SINGAPORE TOKYO MELBOURNE
AUCKLAND IBADAN GABORONE
JOHANNESBURG

Designed by Sue Clarke
Colour reproduction by Track QSP

Printed and bound in Hong Kong

99 98 97 96 95
10 9 8 7 6 5 4 3 2 1

ISBN 0 431 06948 4

British Library Cataloguing in Publication Data
Erricker, Clive
   Buddhist Festivals. – (Celebrate Series)
   I. Title II. Erricker, Jane III. Series
   294.3436

Acknowledgements
The Publishers would like to thank the following for
permission to reproduce photographs.

Zefa Pictures: p.4; Mohamed Ansar/Impact Photos: p.5;
Topham Picturepoint: p.6; Zefa Pictures: p.7; Zefa Pictures:
p.10; Clive and Jane Erricker: p.11; Robert Harding Picture
Library: p.12; Clive and Jane Erricker: p.15; Tim Page/Eye
Ubiquitous: p.16; Topham Picturepoint: p.18; Bruce Coleman
Ltd: p.19; Tim Page/Eye Ubiquitous: p.20; Tim Page/Eye
Ubiquitous: p.21; Clive and Jane Erricker: p.22;
Robert Harding Picture Library: p.23; Graham Harrison:
p.24; A Bradshaw/Impact Photos: p.25; Robin Bath: p.26;
Robin Bath: p.27; Robert Harding Picture Library: p.28;
Robin Bath: p.29; Aspect Picture Library: p.30;
Robert Harding Picture Library: p.31; John Dakers/Eye
Ubiquitous: p.32; Geoff Howard: p.33; Clear Vision Trust:
p.34; Clear Vision Trust: p.35; Tantra Designs: p.36;
Clear Vision Trust: p.37; Clive and Jane Erricker: p.39;
Clear Vision Trust: p.40; Tharpa Publications: p.41;
Jim Holmes/Eye Ubiquitous: p.42; Zefa Pictures: p.43

The Wesak card on page 17 is reproduced courtesy of
Robert Beer.

Cover photograph © Panos Pictures/Neil Cooper

Our thanks to Denise Cush of Bath College of Higher
Education for her comments in the preparation of this
book.

Every effort has been made to contact copyright holders of
any material reproduced in this book. Any omissions will be
rectified in subsequent printings if notice is given to the
Publisher.

Contents

Who are Buddhists?

This unit tells you who the Buddha was
and who his followers are today.

Buddhist
women
showing
reverence to
an image of
the Buddha.

> ❝ **The Buddha
> was a special person.
> He told us how to live
> our lives. When I sit in
> front of an image of
> the Buddha I try to
> remember the things
> he said.** ❞
> – *Sam*

The Buddha

The **Buddha** was born in Northern India 2,500
years ago. He was the son of a local king and was
called Prince Siddhartha. He left home as a young
man to find out why people suffer. Buddhists believe
he found the answer to this question and taught his
message to others. They believe that Siddhartha had
managed to do something that no-one else had
done, and they gave him the title of Buddha, 'the
fully enlightened one'.

Buddhists bowing to the Buddha at a shrine in England to show their respect.

The Three Jewels

A jewel is a very precious thing. It is beautiful and priceless. Sometimes it can be a rare stone like a diamond that has been shaped so that it is almost perfect. But the most precious things in the world are not objects at all. They may be people we love and qualities we treasure like kindness and generosity, which make us happy. When Buddhists speak about the **Three Jewels** they mean the three things that matter most to them. The first Jewel is the Buddha, who is their teacher. The second Jewel is the teaching he gave, which is called the **Dhamma**. This word means 'the truth' and it tells Buddhists how to live their lives in the best way possible. The third Jewel is the **Sangha**, which means 'the community'. All Buddhists think of themselves as part of a whole community of people across the world who help each other to live truthful lives. Sometimes they call each other spiritual friends.

The Buddha told his followers that if they joined together and followed his teachings, they would eventually become just like him, perfect human beings. This is why the Buddha, Dhamma and Sangha are so important to Buddhists and why they call them the Three Jewels.

Becoming a Buddhist

When someone becomes a Buddhist, they will go through a short ceremony. This is a special occasion when they say out loud, in front of other Buddhists, that they take the Buddha as their guide, that they will follow his teachings, and that they wish to be part of the Buddhist community. This is called 'going for refuge'.

The Buddhist Community

This unit explains the kind of life Buddhists' lead.

The Five Precepts

All Buddhists try to live their lives by following five **precepts** or rules that the **Buddha** gave them. These are:

• Not to take life or harm intentionally.
• Not to take anything not freely given.
• Not to be unfaithful.
• Not to speak falsely.
• Not to take drugs that lead to carelessness.

These Buddhist children explain how important the precepts are and how difficult it sometimes is to follow them.

> **The Buddha taught us the precepts and we try to remember these. The fourth precept is about how we speak. Speech is very important in life. We shouldn't speak without thinking because it is a great gift. Sometimes following the precepts is very difficult. Hurting a living animal may be necessary and sometimes in medicine we have to hurt people to save their life when they have a disease.**
>
> – *Sam*

> **When you hurt someone you may hurt them inside without meaning to by saying something or even stealing. You may think it's not stealing but different people have different ways of thinking what is stealing. Maybe borrowing without asking, you may think, is not stealing but they might. Sometimes it's very hard to keep the rule because we sometimes don't understand someone else's idea of what stealing and hurting is.**
>
> – *Polly*

*Monks
listening to a
teaching in a
monastery.*

Monks and nuns

Monks and nuns live in monasteries, where they are expected to remember the Buddha's teaching and the way of life he wanted them to live. They have a special set of rules called the Vinaya. These include the five precepts that ordinary people follow, and five more:

- Not to eat at the wrong time. Normally this means after midday. Monks and nuns only have one meal a day.
- Not to dance or sing.
- Not to wear jewellery or perfume.
- Not to sleep too much or in too comfortable a bed.
- Not to handle money.

They believe that by following these extra rules their lives will be more simple and they can concentrate on religious things. Sometimes they stay up all night **meditating**. Much of their time is spent in silence, trying to have a quiet mind, because the Buddha taught that only a quiet mind will be peaceful and only a peaceful mind can give to others. They try to be a good example to other people.

Buddhist festivals around the world

This unit describes the way Buddhists celebrate their special days.

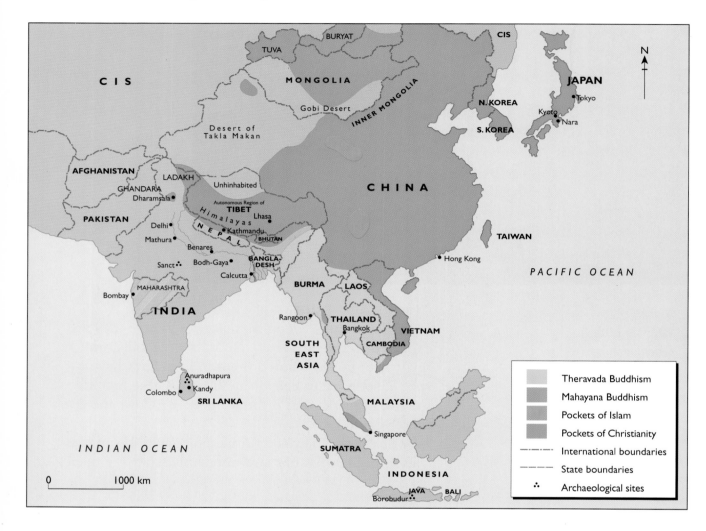

Buddhist countries in Asia.

Buddhists celebrate festivals all over the world but especially in Asian countries where Buddhists have lived for a long time.

Different types of Buddhism

There are two main types or traditions of Buddhism: **Theravada** (meaning the Way of the Elders) and **Mahayana** (meaning The Great Way). Monks and nuns in these traditions wear different robes. Theravada Buddhists, who mainly live in south-east Asian countries, wear saffron or brown robes.

Mahayana Buddhists mostly live in Nepal, Tibet and Japan. Tibetan monks and nuns wear maroon robes with gold and in Japan their robes are usually black. In Europe, America and Australia there is a Western Buddhist Order whose members do not wear robes.

In this book we shall be looking at the festivals of these different branches of Buddhism. They are shown on the chart below. The ones coloured brown are Theravada, the Tibetan ones are maroon and the Japanese ones are black to match the colours of the robes. For the Western Buddhist Order gold stands for the **Buddha**, blue for the **Dharma** (Theravada Buddhists spell this 'dhamma') and red for the **Sangha**. There is a festival day for each of these, shown in these colours.

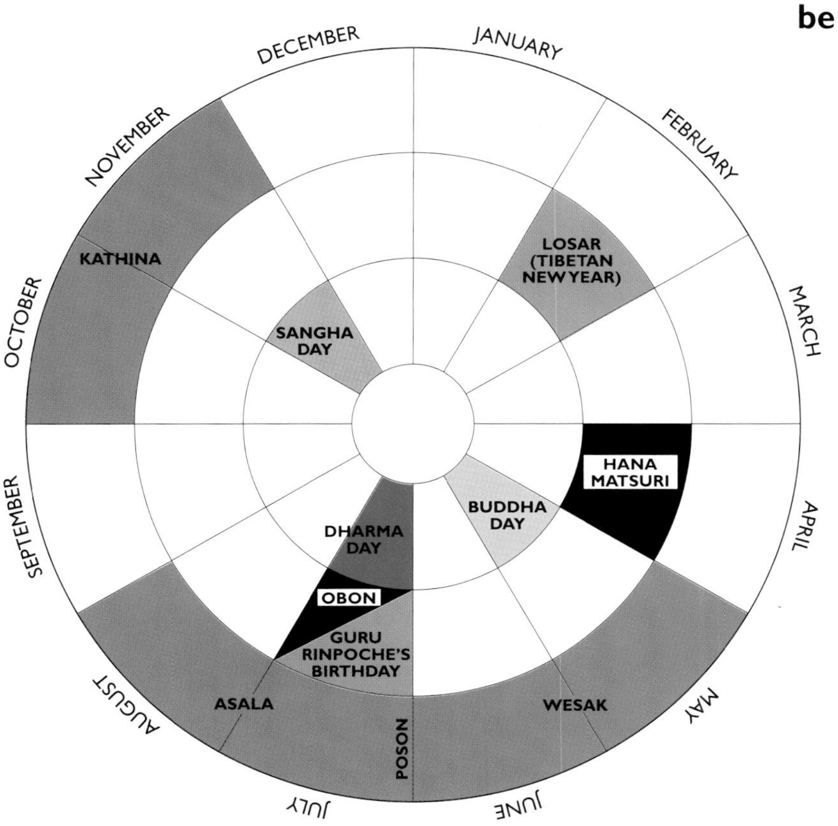

> **What I enjoyed most was lunch because it was all different food cooked by other people and it was all the food I like and I had a bit of everything and I ate it all. I don't know what I might be when I grow up but I might get married for a few years and then have a change and be a monk.**
> *– Rupert*

Festival times

At festival times most Buddhists go to their local monasteries or temples to be with the monks and the nuns. They celebrate with special meals, decorations and processions. They also bring offerings that they put in front of **shrines**. A shrine has a statue or picture of the Buddha placed on a raised platform. Here they light candles and incense and put flowers on the shrine. This is a way of remembering the teachings of the Buddha and what it means to be a Buddhist.

A calendar of Buddhist festivals.

Outer ring   Theravada Buddhists
Middle ring   Mahayana Buddhists
Inner ring   The Western Buddhist Order

Full-moon days

This unit tells you about the importance of the moon to Buddhists.

> ❝ **The moon is very beautiful, prominent and light. Light symbolizes wisdom and this is the quality of the Buddha. He is like the light which is above us, which we look up to and is always there for us.** ❞
> – *Sam*

The Magic of the Moon

When you look up at the full moon, what comes into your mind? The moon reminds people of different things. There are lots of songs about love and romance that talk about the moon. The moon has fascinated us for centuries: its light, the way it affects the tides and its changing shape make it magical.

For Buddhists the moon is important too. Their year follows the moon's cycle rather than the sun's. This is called a lunar year. Their festivals all happen on full-moon nights. They say that the **Buddha** was born, enlightened and died at the time of the full moon. When they look up at it, this is what they remember.

A monk receives a gift from a Buddhist child in England on a visit to a monastery.

Uposatha days

Every lunar month Buddhists have four days when they carry out religious duties. These are called **Uposatha days** and are rather like the Jewish Sabbath or Christian Sunday. The most important days happen at the time of the full moon and the new moon. On these days ordinary Buddhists will visit local temples or monasteries to join the monks and nuns. They take gifts and food. The community joins in a **meditation**, listens to a talk given by a monk, and they chant some verses from the Buddhist scriptures. They will say the **refuges** and recite the **precepts**. Sometimes they will fast for the day by going without food completely, or maybe just not eat meat or fish. This shows that they want to live a spiritual life and not just enjoy themselves. Buddhists believe that by doing these things they are being good. They call doing good deeds gaining **merit**, so Uposatha days are also called merit days. They believe that by doing good deeds their lives will be calmer and happier and that they will have a better life when they are reborn next time.

Some Buddhists may also do these things on the two quarter-moon days but these days are not as important as full- and new-moon days.

Theravada Buddhists

This unit explains who Theravada Buddhists are and what they believe.

When the **Buddha** died he left no-one as leader to follow him. After a while his followers came together to decide exactly what the Buddha taught. This was then learnt by heart by some monks. Later there was another gathering (council) to decide the rules that monks should follow. There were different opinions and this eventually led to the two main branches of Buddhism that exist today: the **Theravada** and the **Mahayana**.

Theravada Scriptures

The scriptures of Theravada Buddhism were finally written down during the first century BCE at a gathering of monks in Sri Lanka. They used the ancient Indian language of **Pali** and wrote on palm leaves. This collection of scriptures is called the Pali Canon or **Tipitaka** ('the three baskets'). This includes the **Suttas** (teachings of the Buddha), the **Vinaya** (rules for monks and nuns) and the **Abhidhamma** (explanations of Buddhist ideas).

In the Theravada scriptures we find one of the most important teachings for all Buddhists. This is the first talk the Buddha gave after his **enlightenment**, about the **Four Noble Truths** and the **Noble Eightfold Path**.

Theravada Buddhists celebrating a festival.

In the *First Noble Truth*, the Buddha taught that the life we live is unsatisfactory.

In the *Second Noble Truth*, he explained that this is because we always want things that we do not have.

In the *Third Noble Truth*, he explained that if we stop wanting we will be satisfied and happy.

In the *Fourth Noble Truth*, he taught the way to do this, by following the Noble Eightfold Path.

This is sometimes shown as a picture of a wheel with eight spokes. These represent the eight ways in which Buddhists try to lead a better life, by developing morality, concentration and wisdom.

Right concentration – to remain free from all mental disturbances such as worry, envy and anxiety (Concentration)

Right viewpoint – being able to see and understand things as they really are – as unsatisfactory (Wisdom)

Right intention – often called right thought. Being able to direct thoughts in an unselfish way (Morality)

Right speech – to abstain from lying, gossiping or speaking unthoughtfully (Morality)

Right action – to behave in a way that will not bring suffering to others (Morality)

Right livelihood – to maintain a living or job that avoids harmfulness (Morality)

Right effort – making an effort to be mindful of the way things are (Concentration)

Right mindfulness – being able to be aware of all you do in thought and action from moment to moment (Concentration)

Right viewpoint
(WISDOM)

Right concentration
(CONCENTRATION)

Right intention
(MORALITY)

Right mindfulness
(CONCENTRATION)

The Noble Eightfold Path

Right speech
(MORALITY)

Right effort
(CONCENTRATION)

Right action
(MORALITY)

Right livelihood
(MORALITY)

The Noble Eightfold Path.

Theravada festivals

Sri-Lankan festivals sometimes have large processions. They put flickering oil lamps around trees and statues and decorate local temples. They send cards to each other to celebrate the Buddha's birth, enlightenment and death. In Thai and Burmese festivals people decorate the gates and doors of their houses with coloured lanterns, paper flags and palm leaves. At temples people carry lighted candles, flowers and burning incense sticks and chant the scriptures. They give the monks new robes and toy trees with bank notes hanging from the branches.

Dana

This unit tells you what Buddhists believe about giving and sharing.

> **When you put food in a monk's bowl you are making a contribution to their way of life and also showing that you are thankful for what he is giving you: the wisdom and showing you the way in life when you are misguided. You're giving to the monk to help him show you how to live.**
>
> – *Sam*

The Fairy and the Hare

Once upon a time there were four friends in a forest: a hare, a jackal, a water weasel and a monkey. One day they agreed that they should not eat the next day, but give the food they found to any poor creature that they met. The next day the jackal, the water weasel and the monkey all kept their finds to give away. But the hare had nothing to offer anyone.

A fairy called Sakka lived in the woods and she changed herself into an old beggar man and went to see the friends. The jackal, the weasel and the monkey all offered their food but when she came to the hare he told her to build a fire to cook his body. She made a magic fire but it did not burn him. She told him that the kindness of his heart should be known everywhere in the world and she drew a picture of him on the moon.

A child at a Buddhist festival putting food in a monk's bowl.

Giving

Dana means giving. The **Buddha** taught that giving or being generous was a very important thing to do. He said that the more you gave, the less selfish you became. But giving isn't easy, sometimes it means giving up what you really want.

Monks and nuns are called **mendicants**, which means that they must live on the offerings of others, just as the Buddha did, and in return they lead a holy life and give teachings. When Buddhist people give to the monks and nuns they are showing that they value the teachings and example that are being given to them. The people are able to give in return and become less selfish themselves. When **Theravada** Buddhists go to monasteries on festival days like **Wesak,** they take food for the day's meal. The monks have bowls called **alms bowls** and the food is put into them. This ceremony is called **Dana**, or giving. They are not just giving food but something of themselves as well. They hope to become more like the Buddha, or the hare in the story.

Wesak

This unit tells you about the Buddhist festival of Wesak.

Buddhists celebrating Wesak with lighted lamps.

> **This morning was Wesak. We went to the Buddhist monastery and we sat in a tent with loads of cushions and a carpet. There were monks with robes on, they were a toffee brown colour. The monks did prayers and spoke in Pali. I gave the abbot a plant with some food. This man had carved a statue of a snake and the Buddha and he gave that to the abbot too. I took photos of the Buddha image surrounded by plants. Then we had food, especially rice, and coffee to drink. There were a lot of people there.**
>
> *– Polly*

Celebrating Wesak

Wesak is the name of the month when **Theravada** Buddhists celebrate the birth, **enlightenment** and death of the **Buddha**. They believe that all three of these important events in the Buddha's life happened at the full moon of this month.

In the Western calendar Wesak happens in late May or early June. Ordinary Buddhist people go to holy places such as monasteries or temples. They listen to a talk about the Buddha's enlightenment, chant and **meditate**, sometimes all through the night. They make offerings and are given blessings by the monks.

Visakha

In Thailand the festival is called **Visakha**. People come to the monasteries at dusk with lighted candles, flowers and incense sticks. They walk around a **shrine**, **Bodhi** tree or **stupa** in a clockwise direction, three times: once for the Buddha, once for the teaching (**Dhamma**) and once for the community (**Sangha**).

In Burma they have a special custom of watering the Bodhi tree. In this way they show their hope that the Buddha's knowledge will grow in the world.

Sri Lanka

In Sri Lanka they make huge lanterns which are decorated with paintings of the Buddha's life. These hang in the streets and temples. They make small ones to hang in their own homes. Street performers act out scenes from the Jataka tales, which tell of the Buddha's former lives as different animals. Little oil lamps in clay bowls are put around Bodhi trees, stupas and Buddha images and people send Wesak cards to friends and relatives to wish them well.

A Wesak card.

Poson Day and Asala Day

This unit tells you how Buddhists celebrate the festivals of Poson and Asala.

> **When the procession arrives there are bright lights and it makes you excited. There are all these naked flames from the torches which seem very mysterious. The bright colours, sounds and crowds make you feel so alive.**
> – Sam

Mahinda and the King of Sri Lanka

In about 250CE the King of Sri Lanka asked the Emperor Ashoka of India to send a monk to his island so he could hear the **Buddha**'s teaching. The Emperor sent his son Mahinda. The King listened to the teachings and was converted straight away. He then asked the Emperor to send an order of nuns to his country. Ashoka sent Princess Sanghamitta with a branch of the **Bodhi** tree in a golden vase. This was planted on the island at Anuradhapura. Two hundred years later it had grown into a great tree and the city had become a famous centre of Buddhism. Today this city and its monasteries are in ruins but the Bodhi tree survives as the oldest tree in the world and a holy place for pilgrims.

A Poson procession in Sri Lanka.

Poson Day

Poson Day celebrates Buddhism coming to Sri Lanka. It is held on the full-moon day of June or July. The atmosphere is like a carnival, held outdoors in the hot weather. Processions called **peraharas** are organized, with huge floats that carry statues telling the story of Mahinda coming to Sri Lanka. These are surrounded by elephants in colourful coats. Drummers join the processions as they move slowly through the streets, letting off fireworks. The largest celebration is usually at Mihintale near Anuradhapura, where Mahinda first met the King and the Bodhi tree was planted.

Asala Day

Asala Day celebrates the Buddha's first sermon. In Sri Lanka there is also an Asala perahara which is even more spectacular than Poson. It takes place in Kandy, the capital of Sri Lanka, in July or August (the Sri Lankan month of Asala) and lasts 15 days. No monks or nuns take part although they may watch. At the centre of the procession is a famous **relic**, the Buddha's tooth. Possessing this relic made the king the true ruler of the country.

Relics

In the Buddhist world a relic is usually a part of the body or a possession of the Buddha or another holy person. It may be something as small as a hair or one of their bones. These things are usually kept in a **stupa**, *a small conical building especially made to put them in. Stupas then become holy places that pilgrims come and visit.*

An Asala procession.

Kathina

This unit explains why Buddhist monks and nuns wear robes and how the robes are presented to them.

> **I think that the monks just wearing the same robes every day doesn't divert their thoughts. Someone who doesn't live a pure life may spend a lot of time thinking about irrelevant things like what they are going to wear but if you only wear one thing you can put all your attention to something more important like your religion. I think that is a good way of keeping your concentration on your beliefs and not thinking about irrelevant things.**
> – *Sam*

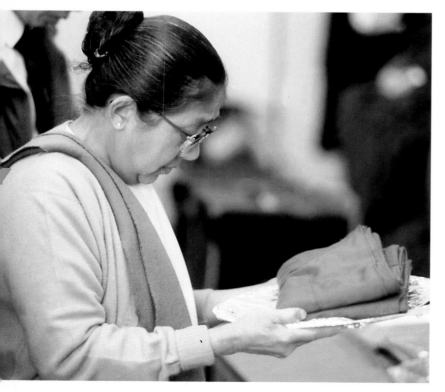

Giving a robe to a monk at Kathina.

Why do we wear clothes?

When we choose clothes to wear we want to look attractive and we want them to suit us. Often we change our clothes when fashions change. Unlike us, monks and nuns never change their style of clothes; they always wear their robes. When monks and nuns chant together in the monastery they say these words to remind them why they wear their robes:

'*Wisely reflecting, to use the robe:*
Only to keep off cold,
To keep off heat,
To keep off the touch of flies,
  mosquitoes, wind, burning and
  creeping things,
Only for the sake of modesty.'

Every year, after the Rains Retreat, when the monks and nuns stay in the monastery for three months, people offer the monks a new robe as a gift. This shows that the monk's way of life is respected and that the monastery is important to the community. There is a ceremony when the cloth for the robes is given to the monks and nuns. It is called **Kathina**, meaning 'difficult', which reminds people that living as a monk or nun and following the **Buddha**'s teaching isn't easy.

The Kathina ceremony

The Kathina ceremony comes during October or November in Sri-Lanka, Burma and Thailand. It is a **Theravada** festival. The Kathina robe is made in a special way. The cloth is bought by ordinary people and in some villages they dye it themselves so that it is a brown or orange colour, just like the robes the Buddha wore. The cloth is given to the monks to cut into shape and stitch together. The robe is then brought to the temple or monastery in a procession and one monk in each monastery is chosen by the abbot to receive the robe. In Thailand the King and royal family give robes. They may visit up to nine temples each year. In Burma it is the tradition for girls to make the monks' robes and at Kathina people also give the monasteries toy trees with bank notes hanging from the branches.

Giving a money tree to the monastery.

Mahayana Buddhists

This unit tells you who the Mahayana Buddhists are and what they believe.

Manjushri, the Bodhisattva of Wisdom.

Just as **Theravada** Buddhism spread south from India so **Mahayana** Buddhism went north into China, Tibet and Japan. As it spread into these different countries different teachings and beliefs developed which gave each branch of the Mahayana its own character.

Buddhas and Bodhisattvas

Mahayana Buddhists follow the **Buddha**'s teachings on the **Four Noble Truths** and the **Noble Eightfold Path** like Theravada Buddhists. They believe there have been many Buddhas before Siddhartha and that there is a future Buddha yet to come called **Maitreya**. They also believe that there are beings called **Bodhisattvas** ('enlightened ones') whom Buddhists can call on to help them on their journey to **enlightenment**. Two of the most important of these are **Avalokiteshvara** (the Bodhisattva of Compassion) and **Manjushri** (who represents wisdom). Tibetan Buddhists hang huge pictures of these figures, called **thangkas**, in their temples and **shrine** rooms and make offerings and prayers to them.

In Japan two of the main branches of Mahayana Buddhism are called **Zen** and **Pure Land**. Zen Buddhists practise silent **meditation** to clear the mind of thoughts. They call this **zazen** ('just sitting'). Pure Land Buddhists chant the name of **Amida** (**Amitabha**) Buddha. They believe that by doing this they will go to his Pure Land, a place with no suffering, when they die, and then become enlightened.

Tibet
If you go to a Tibetan festival it is full of colour. Prayer flags flutter in the breeze: green, blue, yellow, red and white, and everyone happily wears their best, colourful clothes.

The festivals are times for celebrating New Year and Buddhism coming to Tibet, and for honouring their spiritual leader, the **Dalai Lama**. You will see people turning **prayer wheels** as they chant **mantras** or prayers. Today many Tibetans live in other countries because Tibet is ruled by China and they celebrate their festivals wherever they can.

Japan
At Japanese Buddhist festivals the birth of the Buddha is celebrated in spring with flowers surrounding an image of the infant Buddha. Children pour sweet-smelling tea over him to remind them of the perfumed water that the gods bathed him in. Later in the year, during summer, they invite the spirits of dead relatives back into their houses and celebrate this with special dances.

Japanese monks meditating.

Tibetan New Year

This unit describes the Tibetan New Year and explains why it is important to Buddhists.

Tibetan New Year celebrations.

> **If you are a Buddhist one of the things you want to get rid of is the old you when you've not practised well. You would like to change this in the New Year. We try to make our lives purer and more devoted. You want to prove your willpower. You might fast. You wouldn't be extravagant. You go to the temple together and worship. You make a contribution. You give up something that didn't make you the person you think you ought to be. In my character, I think of myself as being too lazy. I need to give up my television.**
>
> *– Sam*

New Year celebrations

New Year is an important time for most of us. We can let our hair down, stay up late to see the New Year in and really celebrate. It is also a time for starting again. We may make New Year resolutions to live a better life and think about the things that we want to do in the future. What was your last New Year resolution? Did you keep it?

New Year is important for Buddhists, too. For Tibetans it is the time of their biggest festival, called **Losar**. Losar starts with the full moon in February and lasts for 15 days. During this time they remember the **Buddha**'s early life and his struggle to preach his message after he became enlightened.

Buddhists spring-clean their homes as a sign that they wish to start again with the New Year. Monks dress up in colourful costumes and masks and perform dances to frighten away evil spirits. People carry lighted torches through their homes and let off fireworks.

Chonga Chopa

On the 15th day of Losar there is a big festival called Chonga Chopa. This is a spectacular celebration with huge sculptures made out of butter of scenes from the Buddha's life. They are coloured with special dyes and prizes are given for the best ones. Monks also hold puppet shows about the life of the Buddha.

A butter sculpture made for Chonga Chopa.

Guru Rinpoche's birthday

This unit tells you who Guru Rinpoche was and what he did.

Padma-Sambhava, the Guru Rinpoche.

Guru Rinpoche means 'precious teacher'. It was the title given to the person who brought Buddhism to Tibet. His name was Padma-Sambhava and because he is one of the best loved Tibetan saints many stories are told about him. Here is one of them.

A story about Padma-Sambhava

When Padma-Sambhava journeyed to Tibet from India he had to cross the huge Himalayan mountains and he went to meditate in a cave high above a great valley. While he was there he met the local King's daughter and they got married. The King was so angry about this that he wanted Padma-Sambhava to be burned alive. The fire was lit but, miraculously, the flames didn't burn him. They turned into water and spilled over to form a beautiful lake. The Tibetans call this lake Tsopema, the lake of the Lotus (a large water lily).

The powers of Padma-Sambhava

Padma-Sambhava is famous for his amazing powers, which he used to control harmful forces and evil spirits. He could change his appearance to look angry and frightening sometimes and at other times peaceful and loving.

Guru Rinpoche's birthday

Tibetans celebrate Guru Rinpoche's birthday in July with a special Tibetan ceremony called **Tsok**. It takes place in a **shrine** room with large colourful pictures around the walls, called **thangkas**. They show **Buddhas** and Tibetan teachers called **Bodhisattvas** ('enlightened beings').

The ceremony begins with food and lighted candles being offered to the Buddha. Monks and ordinary Buddhist people recite the scriptures and chants called **mantras** in order to honour the Buddha and ask for his blessing. This also concentrates their minds. Then the room is still and peaceful while they meditate. They see a picture of the Guru in their minds and they believe that the clearer the picture is, the more like him they will become. Then they will be happier and more peaceful in their lives. To help them they often have their own postcard-sized picture of the Guru to look at.

After the ceremony the food is shared and everyone relaxes together.

Let me light my lamp at your feet
Let the light be shown in my
* wisdom*
To help me help all living beings
Take the road to Nirvana.
(Rinchen Dolma Taring,
Daughter of Tibet, page 130.)

Tsok ceremony in a Tibetan shrine room.

Making mandalas

This unit describes the mandala design and
tells you what it means.

Monks making a mandala.

At all Tibetan festivals they make a design called a
mandala or 'sacred circle'. This represents the
whole universe with all its treasures. These designs
are wonderful works of art but they are also
offerings. They are gifts to the Buddha.

Monks train for many years so that they can make
these beautiful shapes out of coloured sand.
Creating them takes many hours because they are so
complicated and no mistakes must be made. They
are usually made on a low table or a wooden
platform on the ground, like the one in the picture.
Sometimes several monks work on them at the same
time and while they work other monks say **mantras**
or prayers.

When the festival is over the mandala is destroyed
because it has served its purpose.

Making your own mandala

Here a child explains how she makes her own mandala.
'I draw a circle on a big piece of paper and put it on the ground in front of me. Sitting quietly and comfortably I just look at it and let my eyes follow the circle round. Then I close my eyes and think of someone close to me who I'm really fond of. I see the person as clearly as I can and put the person in the circle with my imagination. Now I walk round the circle in my mind. I remember what it is like to be with the person and think of the reasons why I am so fond of him or her. I imagine the reasons are flowers and throw them down around the circle as I walk it in my mind. Then I open my eyes. Now I draw the person in my circle, or something that reminds me of that person, and the flowers around it. Next to each flower I put one thing I have remembered about the person in my circle.'

The completed design of a mandala.

The design of a mandala

Here is a design for making a mandala. Around the outside is a large circle. Inside this is a square with four gates or entrances. Inside that is a smaller circle, which is the mandala's centre. At the heart of the mandala there will be a **Bodhisattva** or **Buddha**, who has a special quality like wisdom or kindness.

Using the mandala

The mandala is meant to help Buddhists become more like the Buddha. By concentrating on the quality at the centre they hope to improve that quality in themselves. Sometimes they will walk round the mandala in a clockwise direction, chanting or praying softly or silently. In this way they will forget everyday things and think of what really matters to them. Their minds will become still and clear and their thoughts more beautiful.

Hana Matsuri

This unit tells you how the Buddha's birth is celebrated by his followers.

Celebrating the Birth of the Buddha.

The Story of the Buddha's birth

Once upon a time the beautiful Queen Mahamaya had a dream. She saw a white elephant with six tusks descend from the sky and enter her womb. The gods told her that she was going to give birth to a son who would become a **buddha**. When it was time for the baby to be born, the queen decided to travel to her parents' house. On the way she visited a beautiful garden called Lumbini Grove. The queen started to give birth and so the Buddha was born in a beautiful, flowering garden.

After the birth two streams of water appeared from the sky. One was cool and refreshing; the other was warm and perfumed. They bathed the Buddha and his mother.

The infant Buddha stood up as soon as he was born. He said: 'I am the chief in the world, I am the best in the world. This is my last birth, I will not be born again.'

Children at a family grave.

Hana Matsuri

Hana Matsuri is a Japanese flower festival celebrating the Buddha's birth. It happens on 8 April, which is springtime, when the cherry blossom is in flower. People set up stalls and hold fêtes to sell food, do folk dancing and watch acrobats. In the grounds of the temples there are displays to remind people of the story. They make papier-mâché elephants to remember the queen's dream and statues of the infant Buddha decorated with flowers. Children pour scented tea over him to represent the perfumed water that he was bathed in.

Higan

Hana Matsuri follows the spring equinox on 21 March, which is called **Higan**, meaning 'further shore'. At this time they remember dead relatives, go to family graves and have Buddhist scriptures recited for them. They offer incense and flowers and pour water over the stone memorials. In this way they remember that their dead relatives have gone to a better life. They remember that, just like flowers, this life passes and leads on to another.

Obon

This unit describes the festival of Obon,
when people who have died are remembered.

Celebrating the
festival of
Obon.

66 **Grandad is important
because he's family. I get upset
because I never saw him and I
wish I had. I think I would have
liked to talk to him.** 99
– Polly

Remembering ancestors

Obon is the most important Japanese
Buddhist festival. It lasts for three days between 13
and 15 July. It is a time when Japanese families
remember their dead relatives and ancestors. They
invite their spirits back into their homes on the first
day, on the second day they celebrate with feasting
and dancing and on the third day they say goodbye
to them as they go back to heaven.

Maudgalyayana's story

This is a story told about one of the followers of the
Buddha, Maudgalyayana. He had special powers
which meant he could visit other worlds. In one of
his journeys he found his mother in the hungry
ghost land. He was very upset and he asked the
Buddha to help him get her away from that place.
He gave a feast for the Buddha and other monks and
the Buddha saved her by pulling her out with a rope.

This story shows the respect Maudgalyayana had for his mother. Japanese Buddhists are meant to show the same respect and concern for their departed relatives. It is also a way that people can make **merit** for themselves so that their next birth will be a better one. People remember the story by playing tug-of-war during the festival.

A family gathers round a family shrine during the Obon festival.

Celebrating Obon

The spirits are attracted to the family home by putting fresh flowers and herbs on the family **shrine**. Families also light small fires or candles and put out food. In some places, like Hiroshima, they put lights in little boats and float them down the river. In Kyoto they light a large fire on the hillside overlooking the town.

On the second day whole villages gather to enjoy a slow dance which everyone joins in. They make a large circle around a stand with lanterns and musicians. People enjoy themselves, eating food and mixing together.

Japanese Buddhist priests visit people's homes and recite scriptures in front of the family shrine to show respect to the visiting ancestors. It is a busy time for them.

On the last day, when the spirits go, fruit and flowers are offered to the Buddha. The family ask for his blessings on themselves and their ancestors in future lives.

The Western Buddhist Order

This unit tells you about the members of a group called the Friends of the Western Buddhist Order and how they live.

FWBO shrine.

The Western Buddhist Order was started in 1968 by an Englishman called Dennis Lingwood. He became a Buddhist monk and changed his name to Sangharakshita, meaning 'protector of the **Sangha**'. When he returned to Britain he started the Western Buddhist Order and now, with its followers, or friends, it is called the Friends of the Western Buddhist Order (**FWBO**). The difference between these Buddhists and others is that they do not shave their heads or wear robes. They do not live in monasteries but have Buddhist centres, and run their own businesses so that they are self-supporting.

The FWBO now have centres in Australia and New Zealand, India, Malaysia and the USA as well as in Europe and the United Kingdom. In India its members work with people who have been rejected by their society. These people are called 'untouchables'. The FWBO want these people to have a better education and to learn about the **Dharma**. In this way the FWBO believe the untouchables can make a new start in their lives.

The FWBO follow the **Buddha**'s teachings of the **Four Noble Truths** and the **Noble Eightfold Path** but they believe that a new kind of Buddhism is needed in the modern world. They say it is important to use what is good in today's society and relate it to the Buddha's message. It is also important that men and women should have the same opportunities and it is not necessary to become a monk to live life as the Buddha taught. What matters is to be a strong and compassionate person and to make friendships with others who are looking for the truth.

FWBO member painting their emblem; this emblem represents the Three Jewels: Buddha (gold), Dharma (blue) and Sangha (red).

FWBO festivals

In their centres at festival times the FWBO have beautifully decorated **shrine** rooms, which you can see in the photograph. The shrine room has a large statue or picture of the Buddha with flowers, incense and candles in front of it. Order members and families sit in front of it and chant and meditate. In this way they celebrate what the Buddha did and try to be like him. This is called **puja**, a name for a kind of worship or service. By the end of the day everyone hopes to feel calmer and more loving towards each other.

Buddha Day

This unit tells you about the day when the Buddha himself is celebrated.

> **On Buddha Day we remember the Buddha. He had great wisdom. He is a standard for people to live by. We all want to live as well as the Buddha himself. He did everything for a purpose and wasn't selfish. He had a pure life and is someone to look up to. He is a very warm person who we want to be like.**
>
> *– Sam*

Buddha Day is one of the three festivals celebrated by the **FWBO** (Friends of the Western Buddhist Order). It is a very joyful festival because it is the day when they remember the Buddha's **enlightenment**, like **Wesak** in the **Theravada** tradition. The festival is held at the full moon in May and on this day FWBO members meet with their families in a hall or centre decorated with streamers, flags and flowers.

FWBO festival days don't have a set pattern. Each centre decides on its own celebrations, but they often hold services for children. Here is an example of one held on Buddha Day.

The Buddha at the moment of his enlightenment, surrounded by Mara's monsters.

A children's service

At the beginning of the service children and parents sat round a **shrine** with a Buddha image, candles, incense and flowers. One of the Order members told a story about the Buddha and explained what he was like. He showed the children gold-coloured beads which were meant to remind them that the Buddha was so happy that his skin shone like gold. The beads were put on the shrine for the children to take later. He showed a picture of the Buddha sitting peacefully but surrounded by monsters who wanted to stop him becoming enlightened. They were throwing weapons at him but he changed them into flowers. This is shown in the picture opposite.

The children pretended to be monsters and then tried to sit quietly like the Buddha. They sang a song about going on a journey across a lake in a canoe on a full-moon night. They imagined being fearless and free like the Buddha.

My mind is clear
*   and bright,*
Flashing like silver,
Follow the full
*   moon's light,*
Dip, dip and swing.

They did actions to the song, pretending they had a paddle and dipping it in the water.

The service finished with each child going up to the shrine, taking a gold bead and making a secret wish.

Child making a Buddha statue on Buddha Day at an FWBO Centre.

Dharma Day

This unit tells you how the teachings of the Buddha are celebrated on Dharma Day.

66 **I once hurt someone by a slip of the tongue by talking about a delicate subject in their life. They had just split up with someone and I was saying how lucky they were. It made them feel really bad and I felt really bad as well. Sometimes, too, I talk when someone else who doesn't speak knows more than me. Sometimes people talk a lot but don't say anything useful but other people are silent but they have something useful to say.**
– Richard 99

66 **Sometimes I think things and want to share it but I can't find the words to say it.**
– Polly 99

Celebrating Dharma Day

This is the second main festival of the **FWBO**. It comes with the full moon in July and is a time to celebrate the **Buddha**'s teachings and put them into practice. It is related to **Asala** Day in **Theravada** Buddhism.

In the afternoon a story is often read to children and families and then acted out to bring the scriptures to life. Here is an example from the Jataka Tales, which are about the Buddha's former lives as different animals. Can you spot the Buddha in the story and think of ways to act it out?

The guilty dogs

Once upon a time, the King left his chariot, with all the leather harnesses, outside at night. While it was dark the dogs of the palace chewed and ate the leather harnessess. The King was very angry and ordered that all the dogs in the city should be killed. The chief of the dogs, who loved and protected them, was very sad about this and went to see the King. He knew that no city dog could get into the palace and that the royal dogs must be the guilty ones. He explained this to the King and asked why the city dogs were going to be punished. The King asked the chief to show that his words were true. The royal dogs were brought before the King and given food to make them ill. After they had eaten, bits of leather came out of their mouths and the King knew that the chief was right. He ordered that all the dogs of the city be cared for all their lives.

After supper there is a **puja**, which may start quietly with **meditation** and people silently going up to the **shrine** with a lighted incense stick, which they offer to the Buddha. In this way they promise to try to practise the Buddha's teachings.

Children at an FWBO Dharma Day service.

Sangha Day

This unit tells you how the Buddhist community is celebrated on Sangha Day.

A Spiritual Friend...

Is the one who you can depend on,
One who knows you like you know yourself.
One who you can fight with, play with,
Scramble in the hay with,
One you can do nothing and be quiet with.
One you can laugh and cry with,
And one you're never shy with.
Such a friend is the one you can trust
With all your heart,
And to be such a friend to others,
Our sisters and our brothers,
Our fathers and our mothers,
Brings a happiness which will never depart.

Sangha Day is a festival held in November by the Friends of the Western Buddhist Order. It celebrates the friendship and love that people of the Sangha, or Buddhist community, share, all over the world. During the festival there will be readings from the Buddhist scriptures, special food and maybe a firework display.

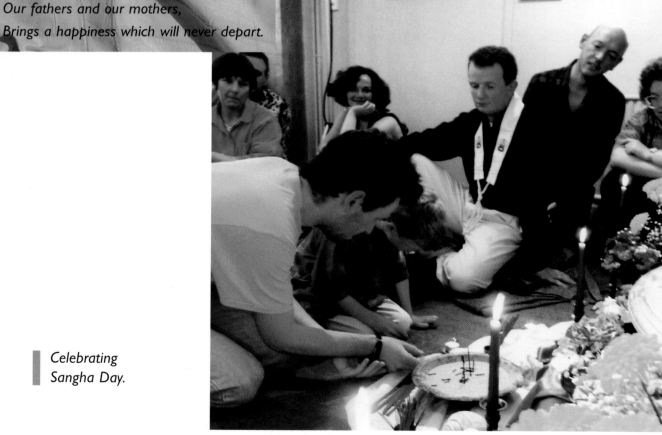

Celebrating Sangha Day.

Loving Kindness

Buddhists try to feel friendship and love for everybody in the world. The **Buddha** called these feelings 'loving kindness' (**metta**). It is not easy to feel like this towards a person who does not like you or who is your enemy, but part of being a Buddhist is to try.

What happens on Sangha Day?

On Sangha Day everyone wears red and the **shrine** room is decorated with red streamers and flowers. For some the day will start at eight in the morning with an early **meditation**. By 9:30am more people will have arrived to meet informally, meditate and prepare lunch. The **FWBO** think it is very important just to have time to talk and share.

The Bodhisattva Avalokiteshvara, with a thousand hands.

In the afternoon they may sit in small groups and share their concerns. They sometimes write these on pieces of paper, put them under the Buddha image and later burn them on a bonfire outside. They may also write down things they wish for themselves on cardboard hands, which they pin on to an enormous painting of **Avalokiteshvara**, the **Bodhisattva** of Compassion, on the wall of the shrine room.

After supper there is a **puja** when all **mitras** (Friends of the Order) renew their vows. They silently offer a candle, incense and a flower at the Buddha shrine. The candle represents the Buddha, the incense represents the spreading of the teaching and the flower represents the fact that things change and die. New mitras make offerings for the first time and people respond by cheering and clapping.

The joy of festivals

This unit looks at the meaning behind Buddhist festivals.

Colourful boats with flags and candles, ready to float on the water.

What's your idea of a really good festival?

Festivals, like birthdays, can be great fun. At Buddhist festivals they have wonderful food, light candles, fly colourful flags in the wind, make boats to float on the water and give each other presents.

" I really enjoyed going to the temple. We heard how a family had come to London from Vietnam. They left in little boats and were picked up at sea. The food was the best thing – so much of it. All sorts of vegetable dishes. We had to eat as much as we could because they had made it specially for us and they wouldn't eat anything left over. It made me feel very special. "
– *Katy*

Friendship

At the heart of Buddhist festivals is the **Buddha**'s message. Be mindful, think carefully about everything that you do and be generous to other people. Perhaps the best thing about festivals is that people who enjoy each other's company meet together. It is a time to share not only the things they enjoy doing but also their friendship. It is good to be with friends, and spiritual friends, ones you are very close to, and are very special to you. They are people you can share your secrets with: your hopes, your dreams, and things you don't feel very happy about. Festivals are times to make you feel better about yourself because you have been with people who value you.

Some Buddhists believe that there is a land called **Sukkhavati** where you go when you die. 'Sukkha' means 'happiness' and 'vati' means 'land'. It is a place where there are no bad things, no suffering. There you can forget all the problems in life: quarrels, sadness and all the setbacks that are so difficult to deal with. You can feel good about yourself and give to others.

Perhaps you have a place where you go when you want to feel better – your bedroom or the park, the seashore or a place where you meet your friends and talk. Some people think Sukkhavati must be a bit like these places and Buddhist festivals give Buddhists a taste of Sukkhavati. But Buddhists also think of Sukkhavati as a place inside their hearts where there is nothing but loving kindness or **metta**.

Sukkhavati is thought of as a peaceful place where people can leave their problems behind.

When Buddhists meditate they say:
'May all things be free from suffering,
May all beings live in peace.'

There is a saying that sums up what Buddhists really celebrate at festival times. It is something they try to carry out in their lives:
'Close your eyes and you will see clearly,
Cease to listen and you will hear the truth,
Be silent and your heart will sing,
Be gentle and you will need no strength,
Be patient and you will achieve all things.'

Glossary

Some words are given in Pali (the language of the Theravada scriptures) with the Sanskrit word (the language of Mahayana scriptures) in brackets.

Abhidhamma (Abhidharma) collection of texts explaining Buddhist ideas

Alms bowl the bowl in which a monk or nun receives food

Amida (Amitabha) the Buddha who rules in Sukkhavati (the Western Paradise)

Asala Sri-Lankan month with a festival celebrating the procession of the Buddha's tooth

Avalokiteshvara the Bodhisattva of Compassion

Bodhi enlightenment. The name given to the tree under which the Buddha gained enlightenment

Bodhisattva an enlightened being who helps Buddhists in this life

Buddha 'Enlightened One'. The title given to Siddhatta Gotama (Siddhartha Gautama)

Dalai Lama leader of Tibetan Buddhists. Incarnation of Avalokiteshvara

Dana giving or generosity. Also the name for a ceremony in which Buddhists give food to monks and nuns

Dhamma (Dhamma) the teachings of the Buddha; the truth. Spelling differs between Mahayana and Theravada Buddhists

Enlightenment awakening or seeing the truth. The achievement of the Buddha

Four Noble Truths the Buddha's teaching about suffering or unsatisfactoriness (dukkha)

FWBO the Friends of the Western Buddhist Order

Guru Rinpoche 'Precious Teacher'. The title given to the Tibetan saint Padma-Sambhava

Hana Matsuri Japanese festival of flowers celebrating the Buddha's birth

Higan 'further shore'. A time when Japanese Buddhists remember their dead relatives

Kathina the Theravada ceremony in which a new robe is given to the monastery

Losar Tibetan New Year

Mahayana The Great Way. One of the two main branches of Buddhism

Maitreya the future Buddha

Mandala a circular design used in Tibetan Buddhist ceremonies

Manjushri the Bodhisattva of Wisdom

Mantra a special sound or prayer

Meditation a Buddhist practice for training the mind, making it peaceful and gaining insight

Mendicant a monk or nun. One who receives basic needs from others

Merit good deeds and the reward that comes from them

Metta loving kindness

Mitra a Friend of the Western Buddhist Order

Noble Eightfold Path the fourth Noble Truth explaining the practice Buddhists should follow

Obon the Japanese festival in which Buddhists invite the spirits of dead ancestors back into their homes

Pali the language of the Theravada scriptures

Perahara Sri-Lankan word for a procession

Poson the Theravada festival celebrating Buddhism coming to Sri-Lanka

Prayer wheels instruments turned by Tibetan Buddhists when worshipping

Precepts the rules that Buddhists follow. Five for ordinary Buddhists and ten for monks and nuns

Puja the name for a Buddhist service or worship

Pure Land the 'western paradise' of the Buddha Amida (Amitabha) which Buddhists of the Pure Land School believe they go to when they die

Refuge a place of safety. Buddhists 'go for refuge' to the Buddha, Dharma (Dhamma) and Sangha

Relic a part of the body of the Buddha or a Buddhist saint which is put in a stupa

Sangha the Order or Buddhist community

Sanskrit the language of the Mahayana scriptures

Shrine a place where worship takes place

Stupa a circular building in which Buddhist relics are put

Sukkhavati the name for the Pure Land of the Buddha Amida (Amitabha). A realm of bliss or happiness

Suttas (**sutras**) the scriptures which contain the Buddha's teachings

Thangka a Tibetan Buddhist wall-hanging with Buddhas, Bodhisattvas, saints or a mandala design on it

Theravada Way of the Elders. One of the two main branches of Buddhism

Three Jewels Buddha, Dhamma, (Dharma) Sangha

Tipitaka the Three Baskets. The three-fold division of the Pali canon (the Theravada scriptures)

Tsok a Tibetan ceremony

Uposatha days four days of the month when Buddhists worship. The full-moon day is the most important

Vinaya the code of discipline for monks and nuns

Visakha the Thai name for Wesak

Wesak Theravada festival celebrating the Buddha's enlightenment. Also the name of the month when the festival is celebrated

Zazen Zen meditation meaning 'just sitting'

Zen a Japanese form of Mahayana Buddhism

Further reading

World Religions: Buddhism. Catherine Hewitt; Wayland (Publishers) Ltd, 1995.

Religions through Festivals: Buddhism. Holly and Peter Connolly; Longman, 1989.

Discovering Religions: Buddhism. ed. Sue Penney; Heinemann Publishers (Oxford) Ltd, 1995

Discovering Sacred Texts: Buddhist Scriptures. Anil Goonewardene; Heinemann Publishers (Oxford) Ltd, 1994.

Let's Celebrate Spring. Mike Rosen, ed. Deb Elliott; Wayland (Publishers) Ltd, 1994.

Let's Celebrate Summer. Mike Rosen, ed. Deb Elliott; Wayland (Publishers) Ltd, 1994.

Let's Celebrate Autumn. Mike Rosen, ed. Deb Elliott; Wayland (Publishers) Ltd, 1994.

Let's Celebrate Winter. Mike Rosen, ed. Deb Elliott; Wayland (Publishers) Ltd, 1994.

Understanding Religions: Food and Fasting. Deidre Burke, Wayland (Publishers) Ltd, 1992.

Understanding Religions: Pilgrimages and Journeys. Katherine Prior, Wayland (Publishers) Ltd, 1992.

A closer look

This picture shows Theravada Buddhists celebrating a festival. In Sri-Lanka, Buddhist festivals sometimes have large processions. Oil lamps are put around trees and statues and local temples are decorated. In Thailand and Burma, the gates and doors of houses are decorated with coloured lanterns, paper flags and palm leaves. People celebrate the Buddha's birth, enlightenment and death.

Index